TABLE OF CONTENTS

SECTION 1

SECTION 2

SECTION 3

SECTION 4

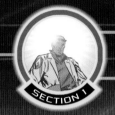

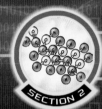

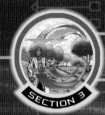

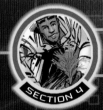

SECTION 1 FOOD FROM THE SUN

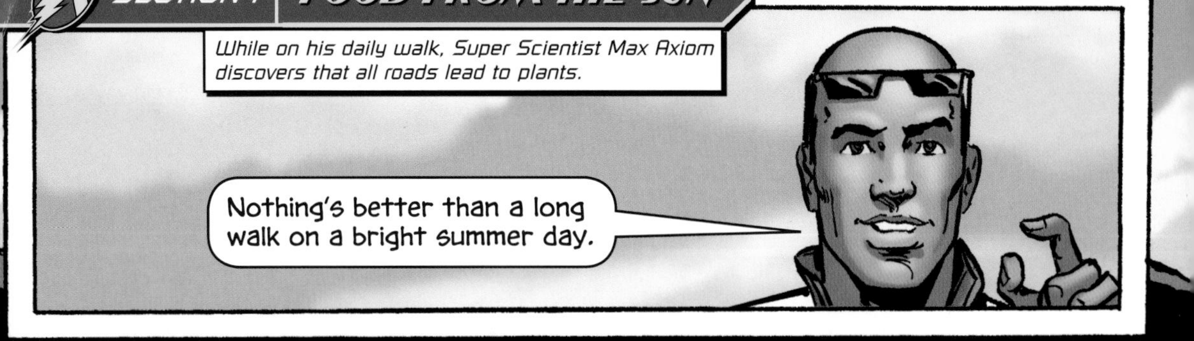
While on his daily walk, Super Scientist Max Axiom discovers that all roads lead to plants.
Nothing's better than a long walk on a bright summer day.

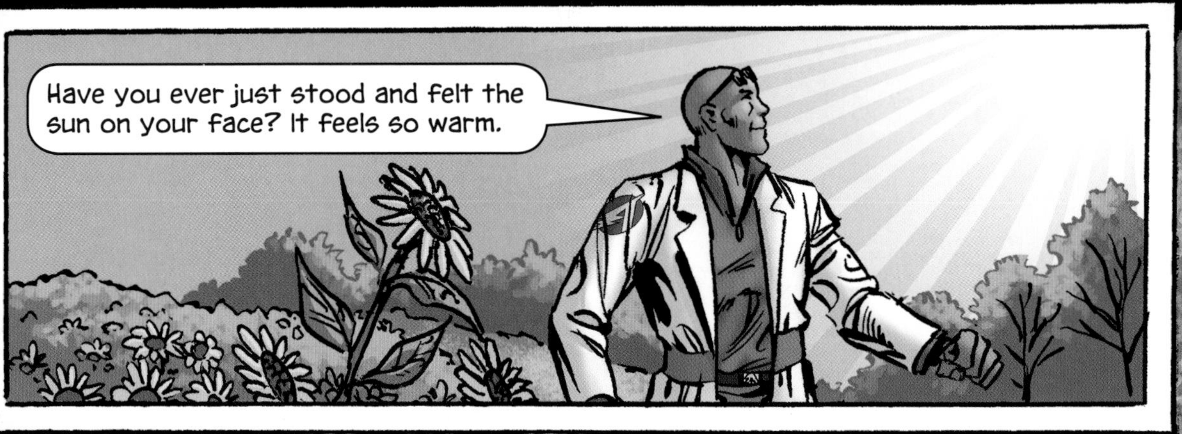
Have you ever just stood and felt the sun on your face? It feels so warm.

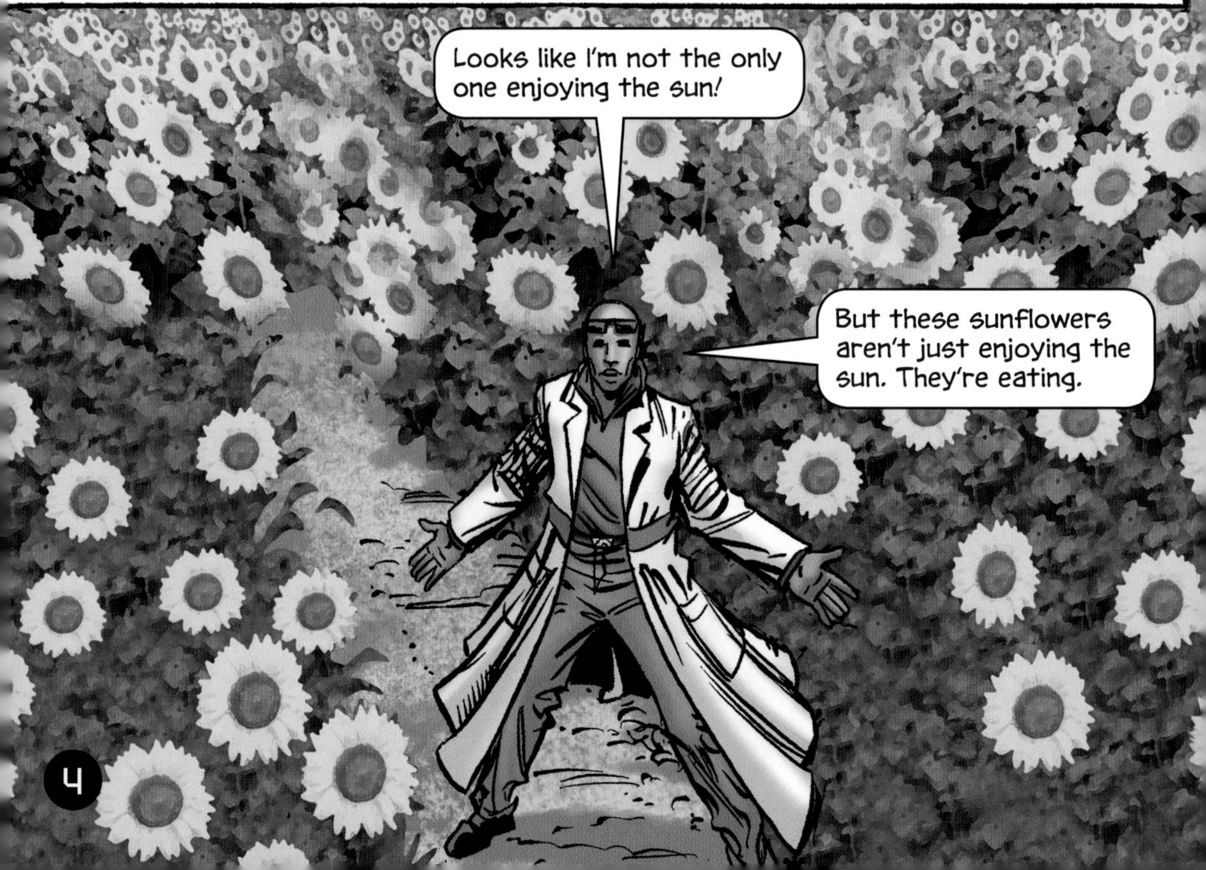
Looks like I'm not the only one enjoying the sun!
But these sunflowers aren't just enjoying the sun. They're eating.

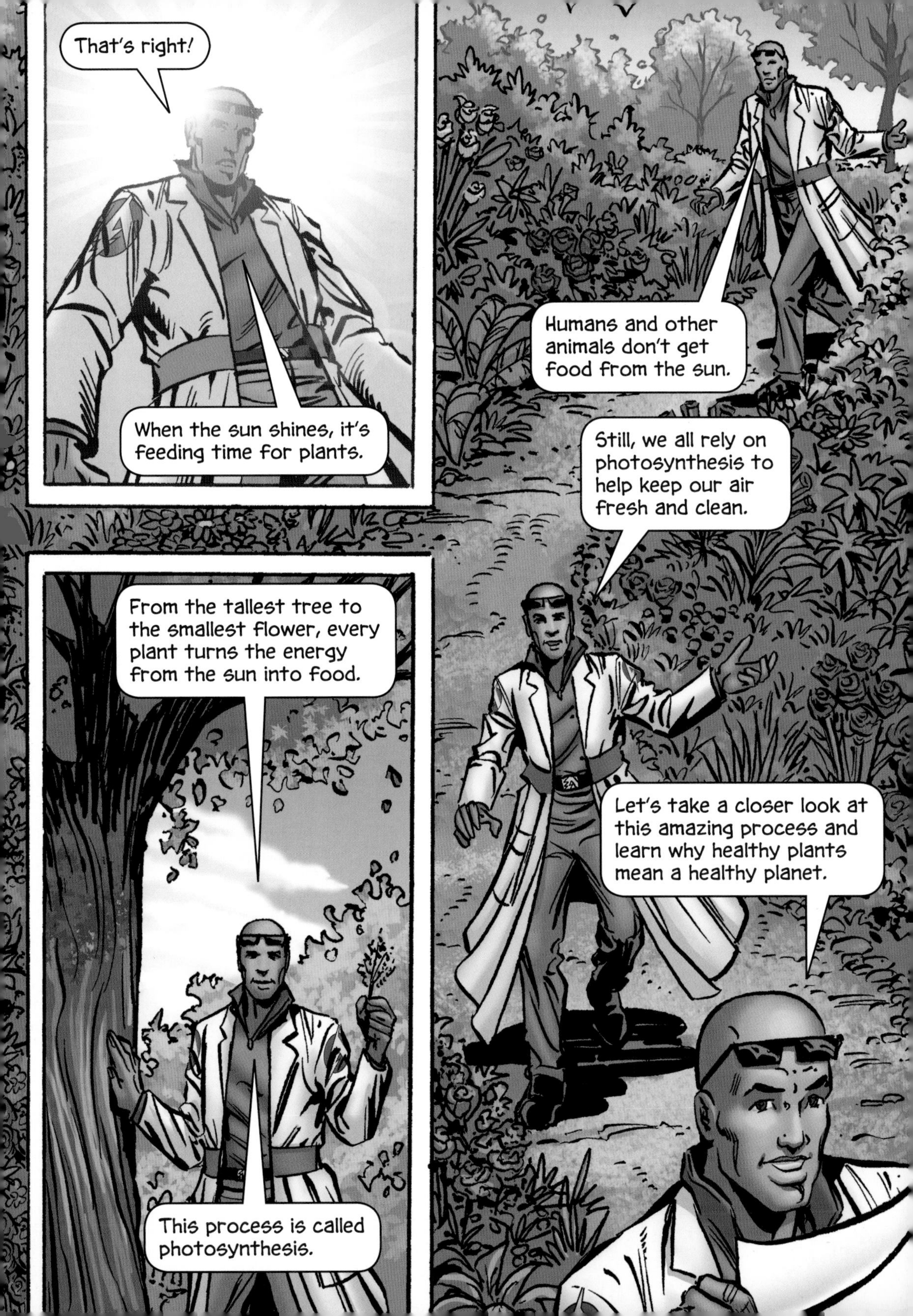
That's right!
When the sun shines, it's feeding time for plants.
From the tallest tree to the smallest flower, every plant turns the energy from the sun into food.
This process is called photosynthesis.
Humans and other animals don't get food from the sun.
Still, we all rely on photosynthesis to help keep our air fresh and clean.
Let's take a closer look at this amazing process and learn why healthy plants mean a healthy planet.

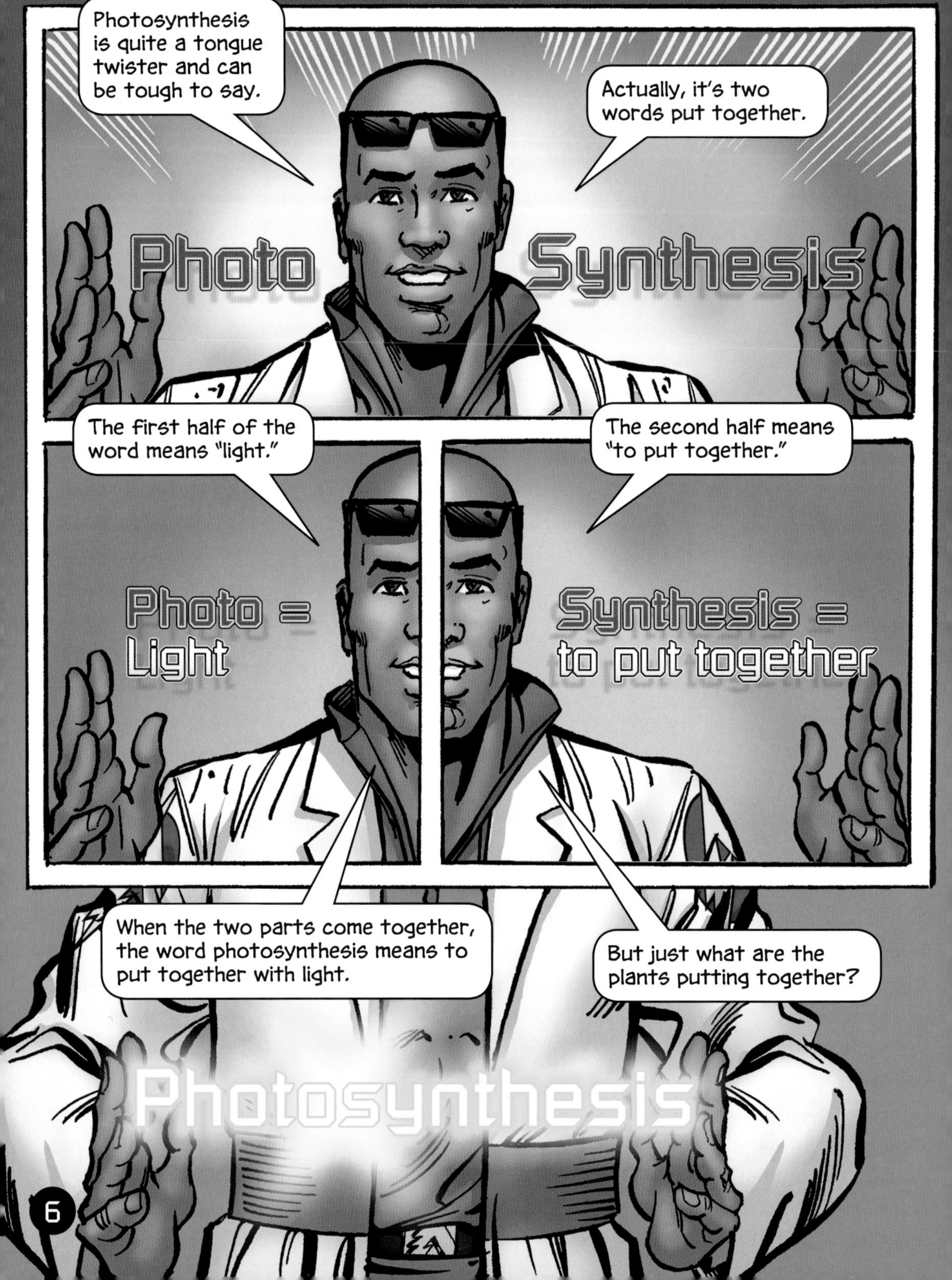
Photosynthesis is quite a tongue twister and can be tough to say.
Actually, it's two words put together.
Photo
Synthesis
The first half of the word means "light."
The second half means "to put together."
Photo = Light
Synthesis = to put together
When the two parts come together, the word photosynthesis means to put together with light.
But just what are the plants putting together?
Photosynthesis

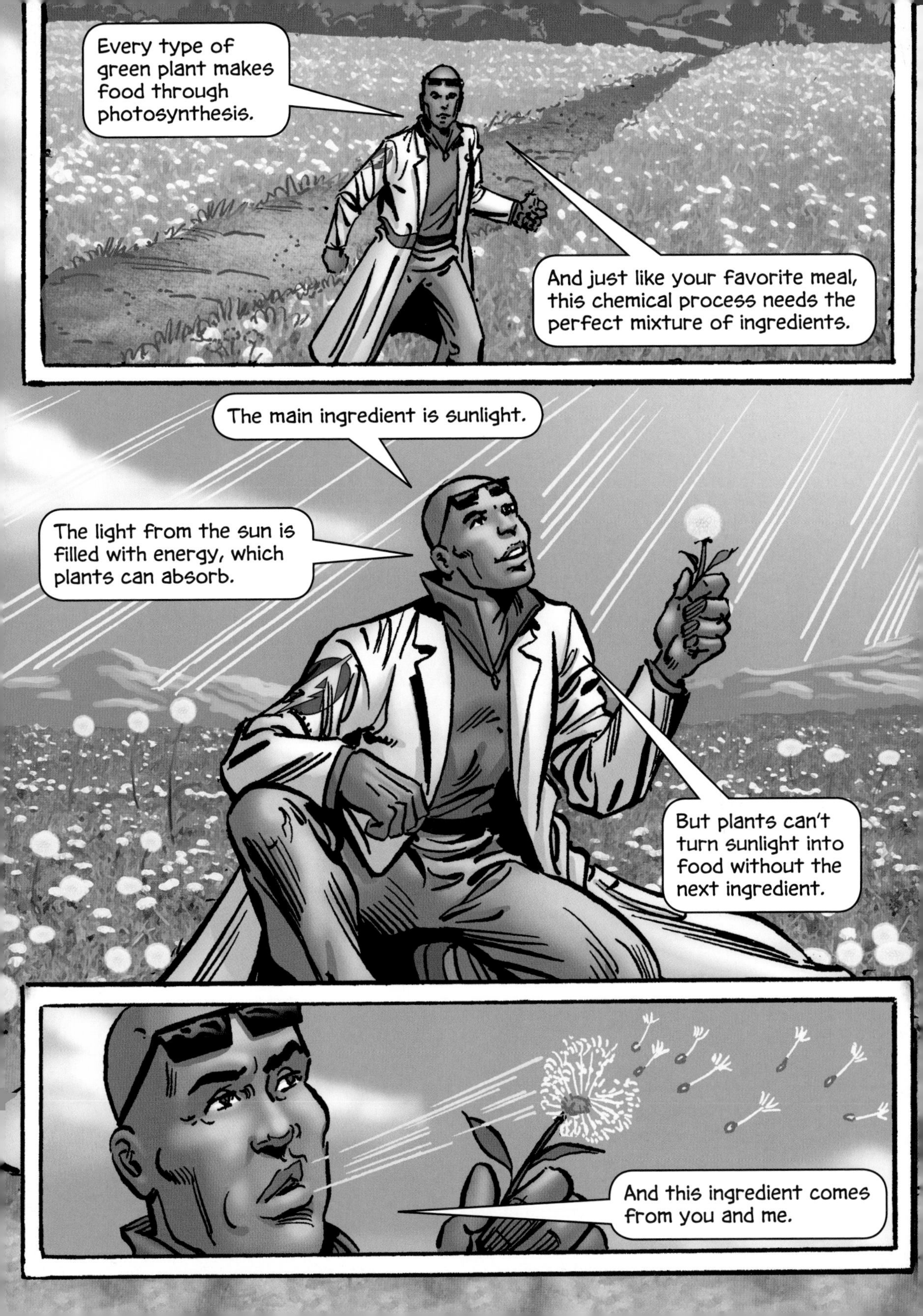
Every type of green plant makes food through photosynthesis.
And just like your favorite meal, this chemical process needs the perfect mixture of ingredients.
The main ingredient is sunlight.
The light from the sun is filled with energy, which plants can absorb.
But plants can't turn sunlight into food without the next ingredient.
And this ingredient comes from you and me.

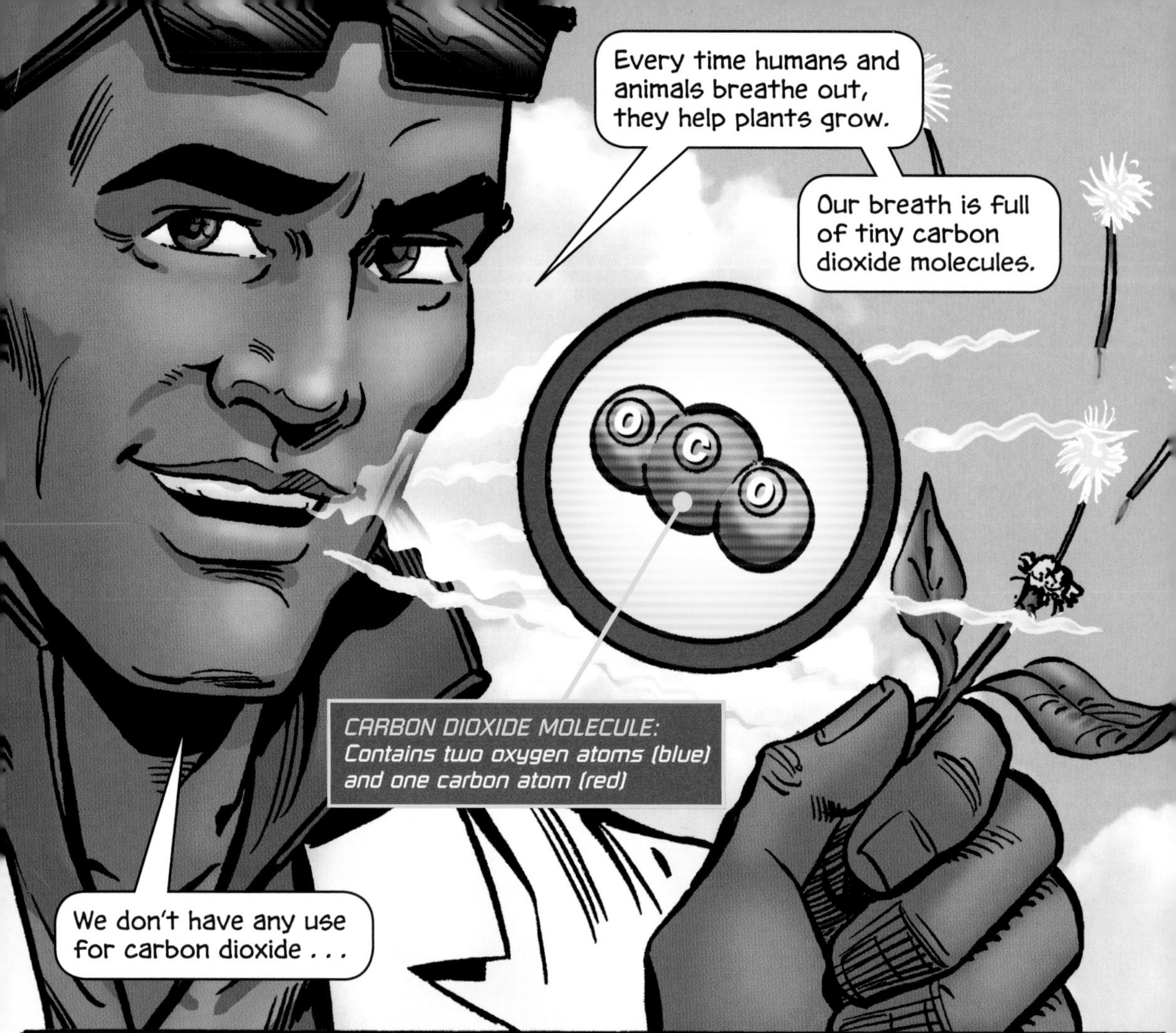
Every time humans and animals breathe out, they help plants grow.
Our breath is full of tiny carbon dioxide molecules.
O
C
O
CARBON DIOXIDE MOLECULE: Contains two oxygen atoms (blue) and one carbon atom (red)
We don't have any use for carbon dioxide . . .

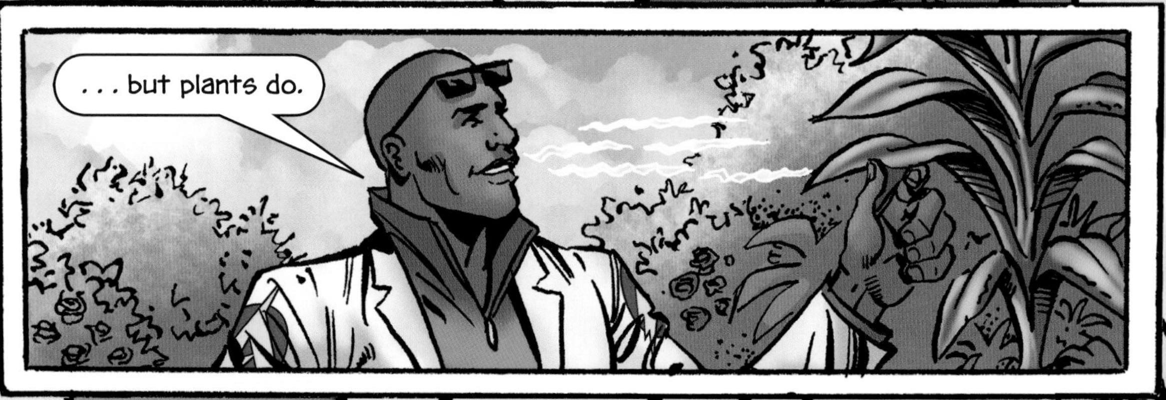
. . . but plants do.

DEFINITION

carbon dioxide (KAHR-buhn dye-AHK-side)
A colorless, odorless gas that people and animals breathe out.

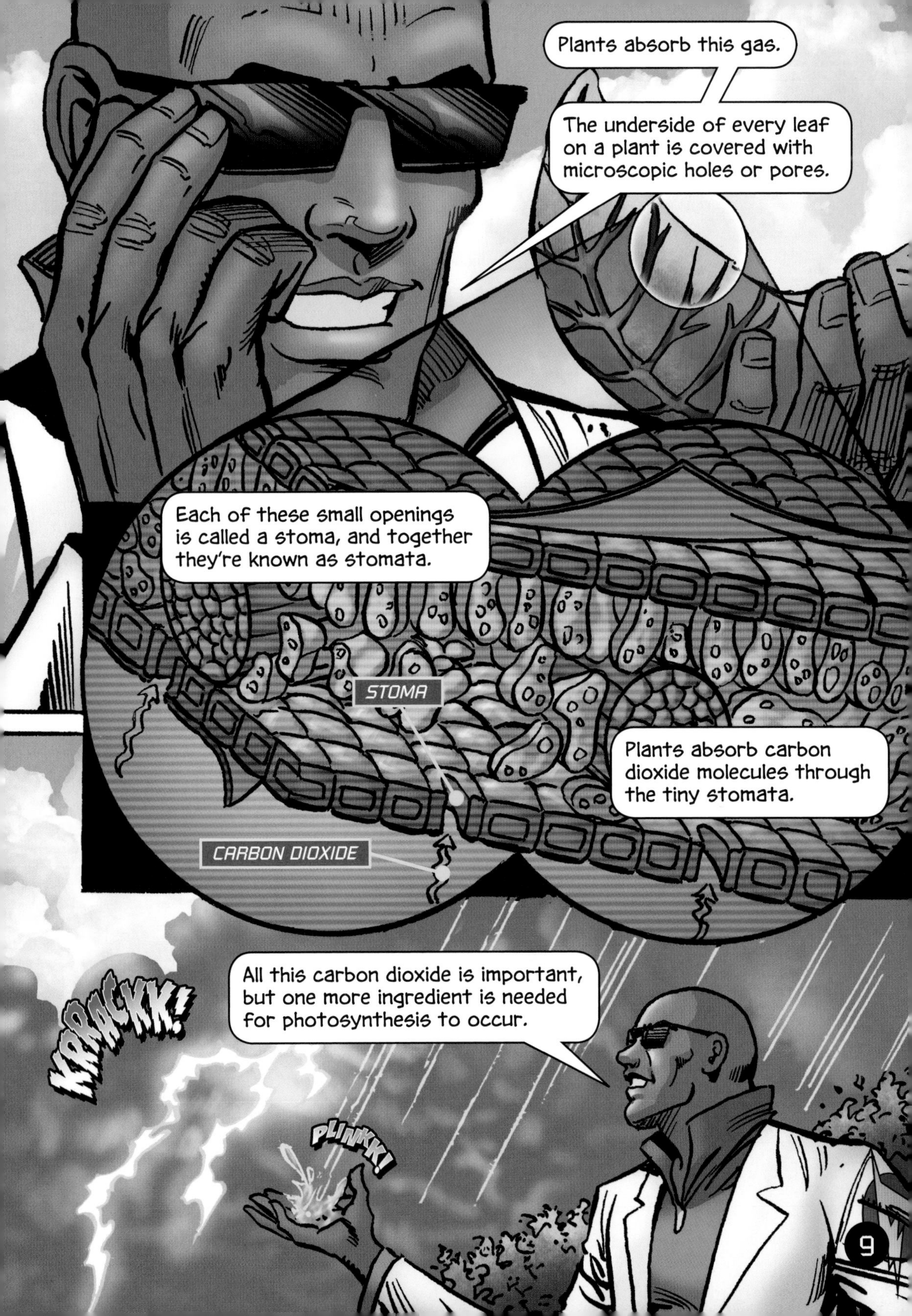

Plants absorb this gas.
The underside of every leaf on a plant is covered with microscopic holes or pores.
Each of these small openings is called a stoma, and together they're known as stomata.
STOMA
Plants absorb carbon dioxide molecules through the tiny stomata.
CARBON DIOXIDE
All this carbon dioxide is important, but one more ingredient is needed for photosynthesis to occur.
KRRACKK!
PLINKK!

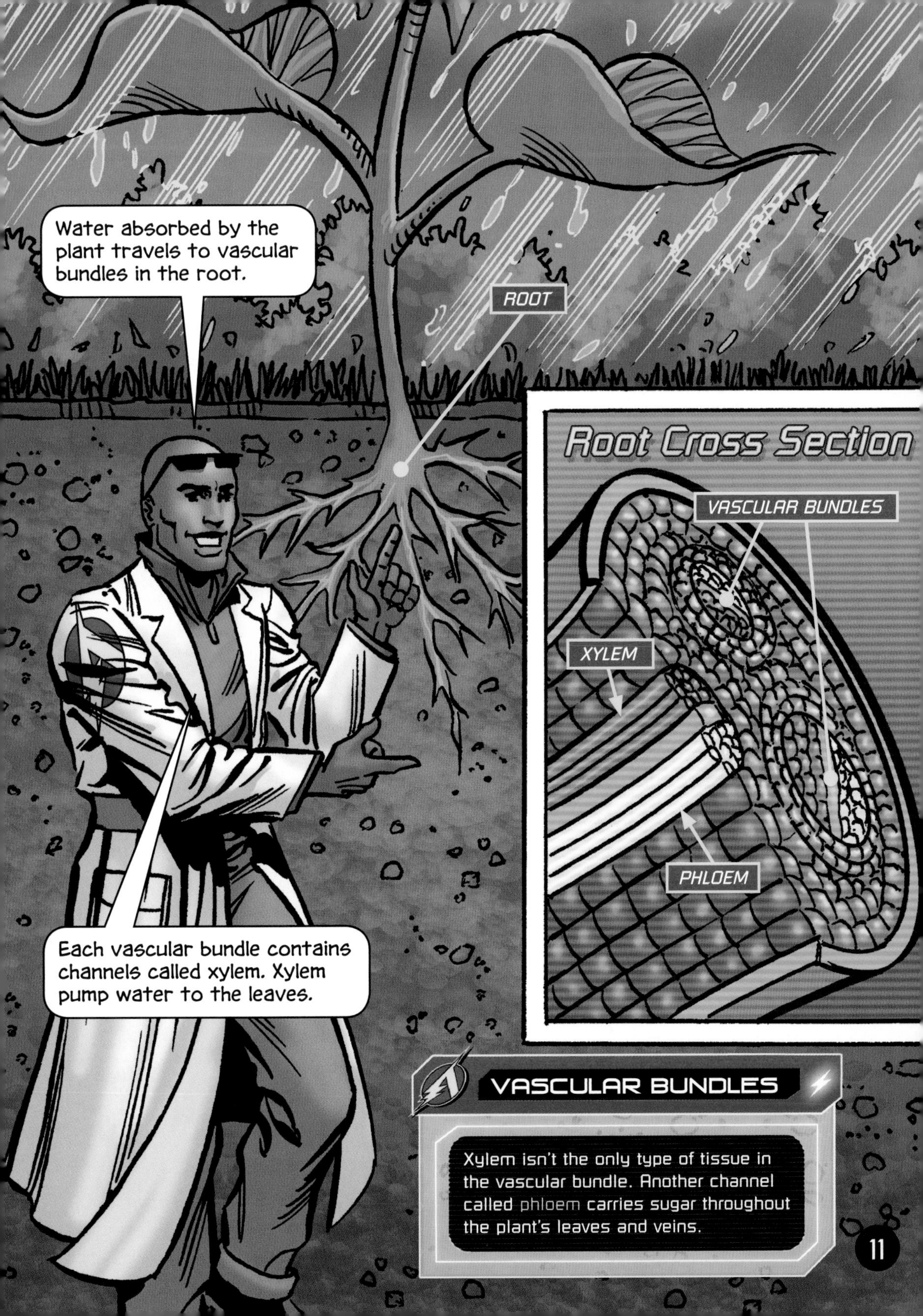

Water absorbed by the plant travels to vascular bundles in the root.
ROOT
Root Cross Section
VASCULAR BUNDLES
XYLEM
PHLOEM
Each vascular bundle contains channels called xylem. Xylem pump water to the leaves.

VASCULAR BUNDLES

Xylem isn't the only type of tissue in the vascular bundle. Another channel called phloem carries sugar throughout the plant's leaves and veins.

Plants need the water in these channels to start the process of photosynthesis.

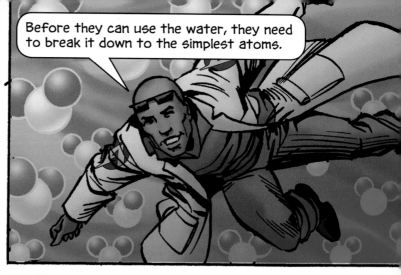

Before they can use the water, they need to break it down to the simplest atoms.

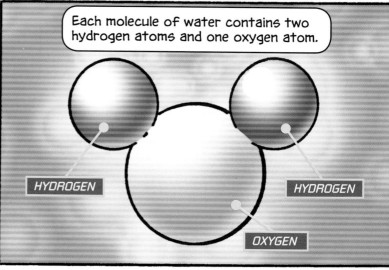

Each molecule of water contains two hydrogen atoms and one oxygen atom.

HYDROGEN

HYDROGEN

OXYGEN

To see where plants take apart water molecules, let's jump inside a plant cell.

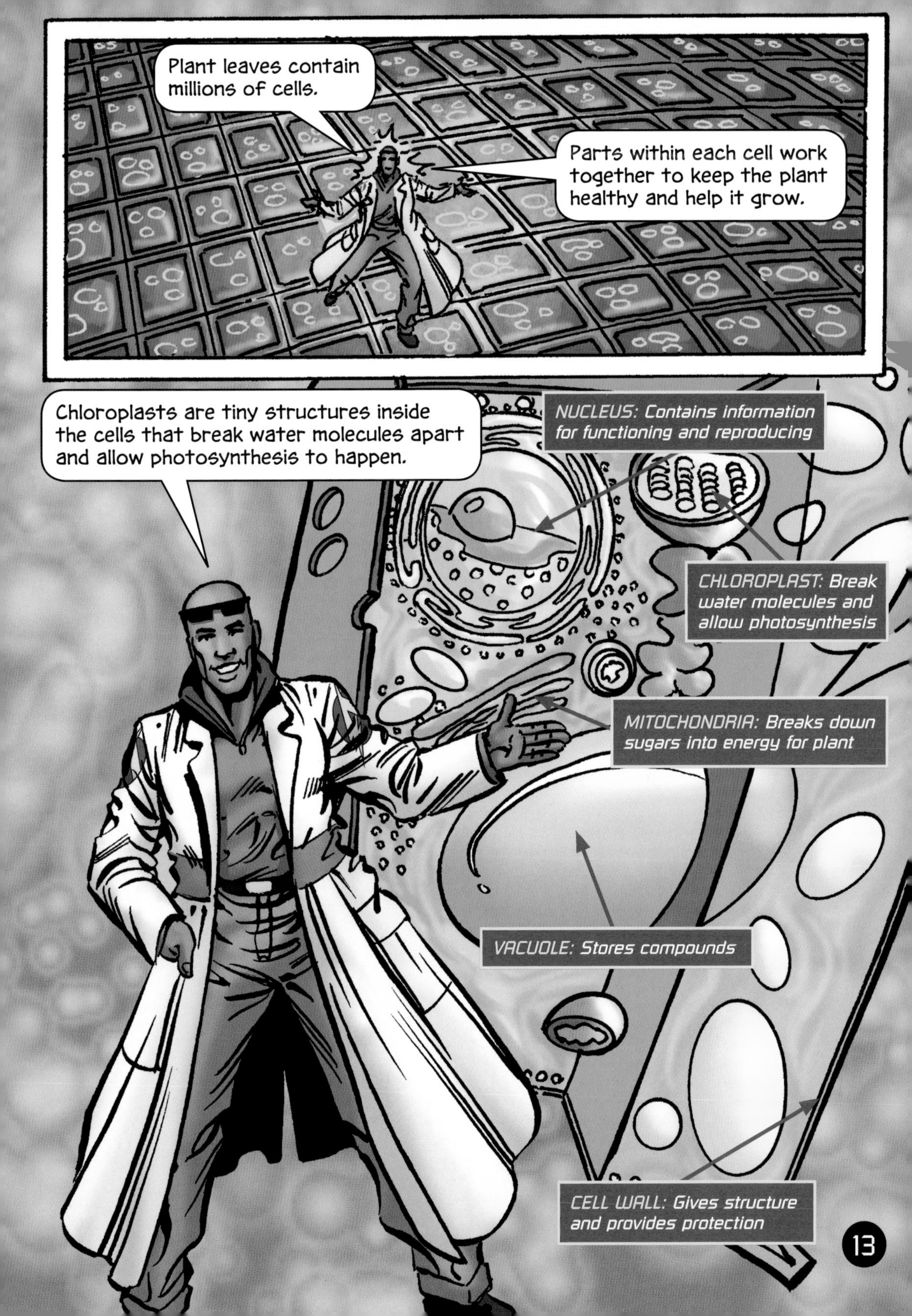

Plant leaves contain millions of cells.
Parts within each cell work together to keep the plant healthy and help it grow.
Chloroplasts are tiny structures inside the cells that break water molecules apart and allow photosynthesis to happen.
NUCLEUS: Contains information for functioning and reproducing
CHLOROPLAST: Break water molecules and allow photosynthesis
MITOCHONDRIA: Breaks down sugars into energy for plant
VACUOLE: Stores compounds
CELL WALL: Gives structure and provides protection

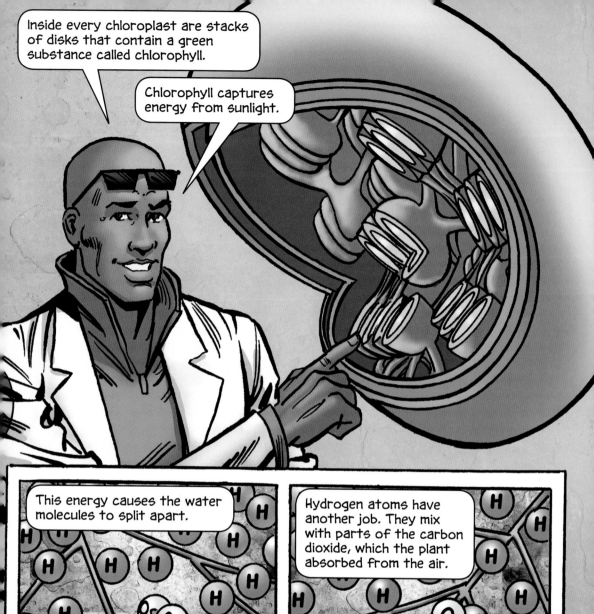

Inside every chloroplast are stacks of disks that contain a green substance called chlorophyll.

Chlorophyll captures energy from sunlight.

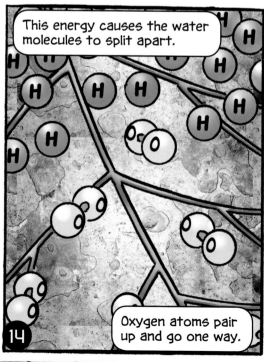

This energy causes the water molecules to split apart.

Oxygen atoms pair up and go one way.

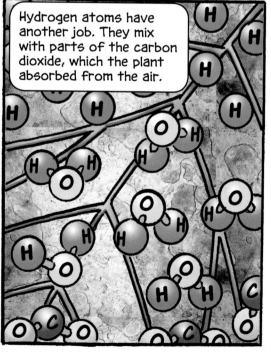

Hydrogen atoms have another job. They mix with parts of the carbon dioxide, which the plant absorbed from the air.

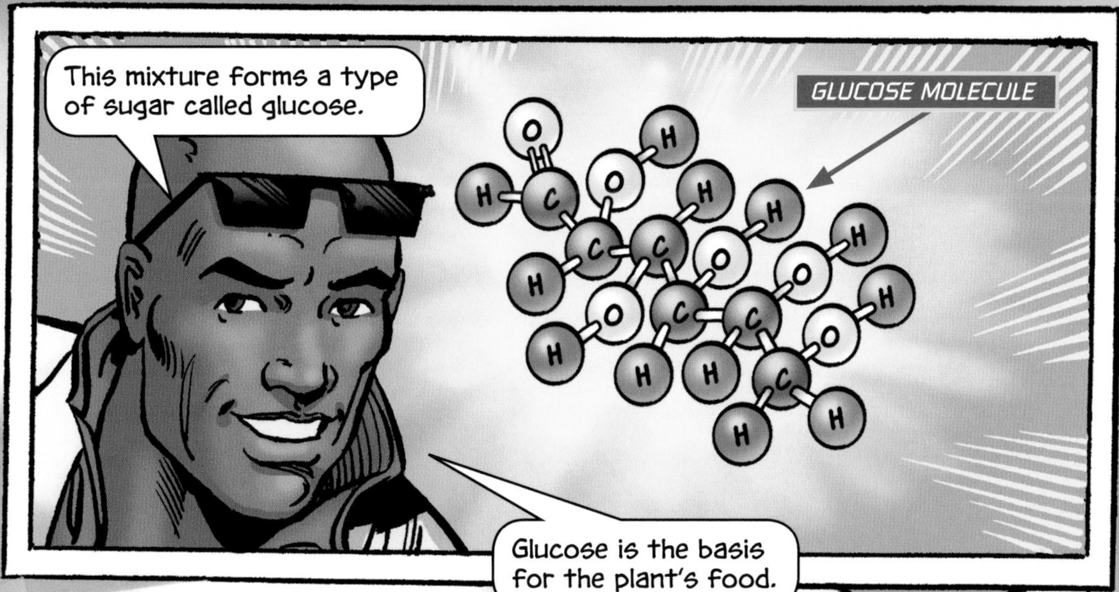
This mixture forms a type of sugar called glucose.
GLUCOSE MOLECULE
O
H
H
C
O
H
H
C
C
O
H
H
O
C
C
O
H
H
H
H
C
H
H
Glucose is the basis for the plant's food.

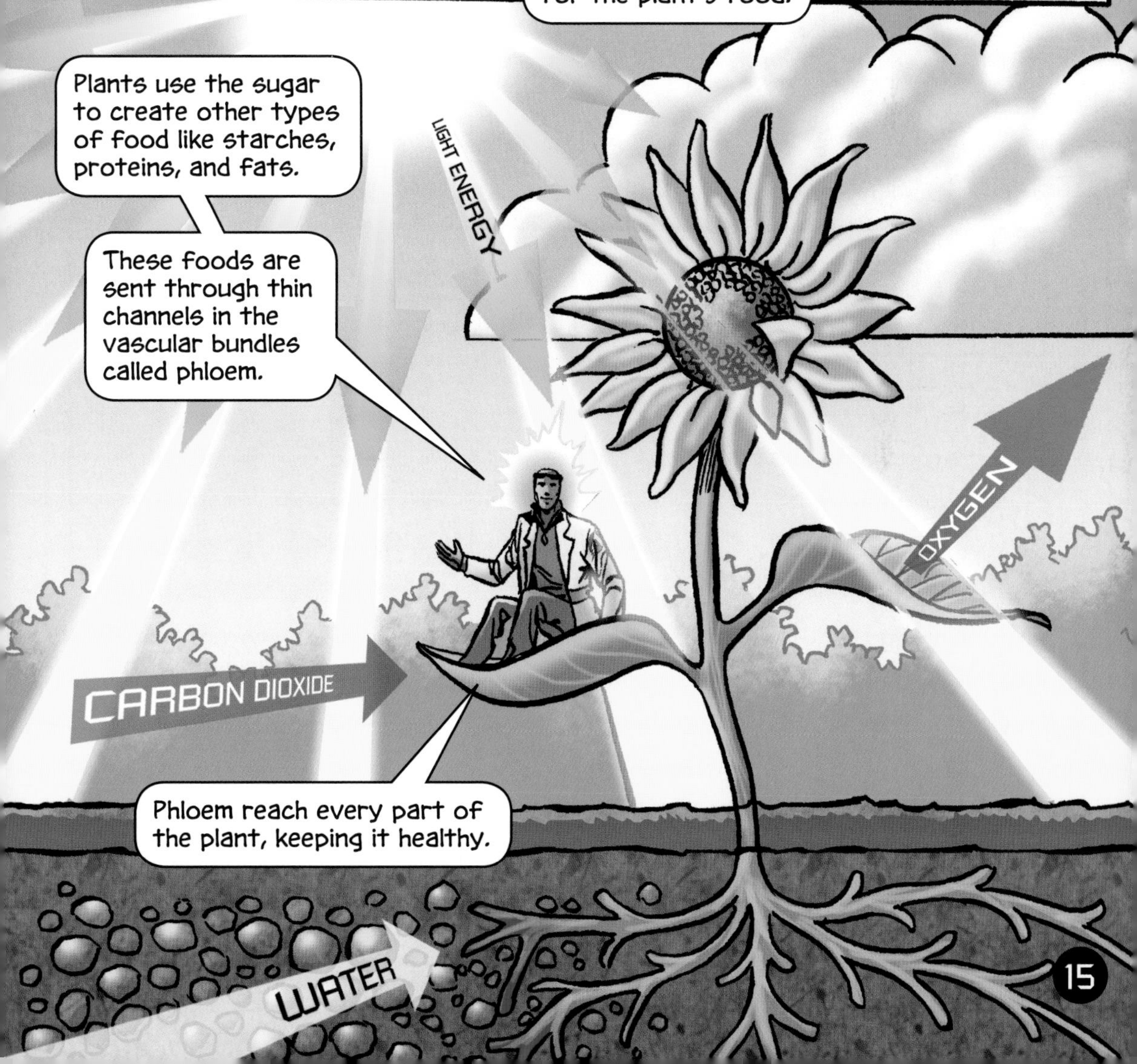
Plants use the sugar to create other types of food like starches, proteins, and fats.
LIGHT ENERGY
These foods are sent through thin channels in the vascular bundles called phloem.
OXYGEN
CARBON DIOXIDE
Phloem reach every part of the plant, keeping it healthy.
WATER

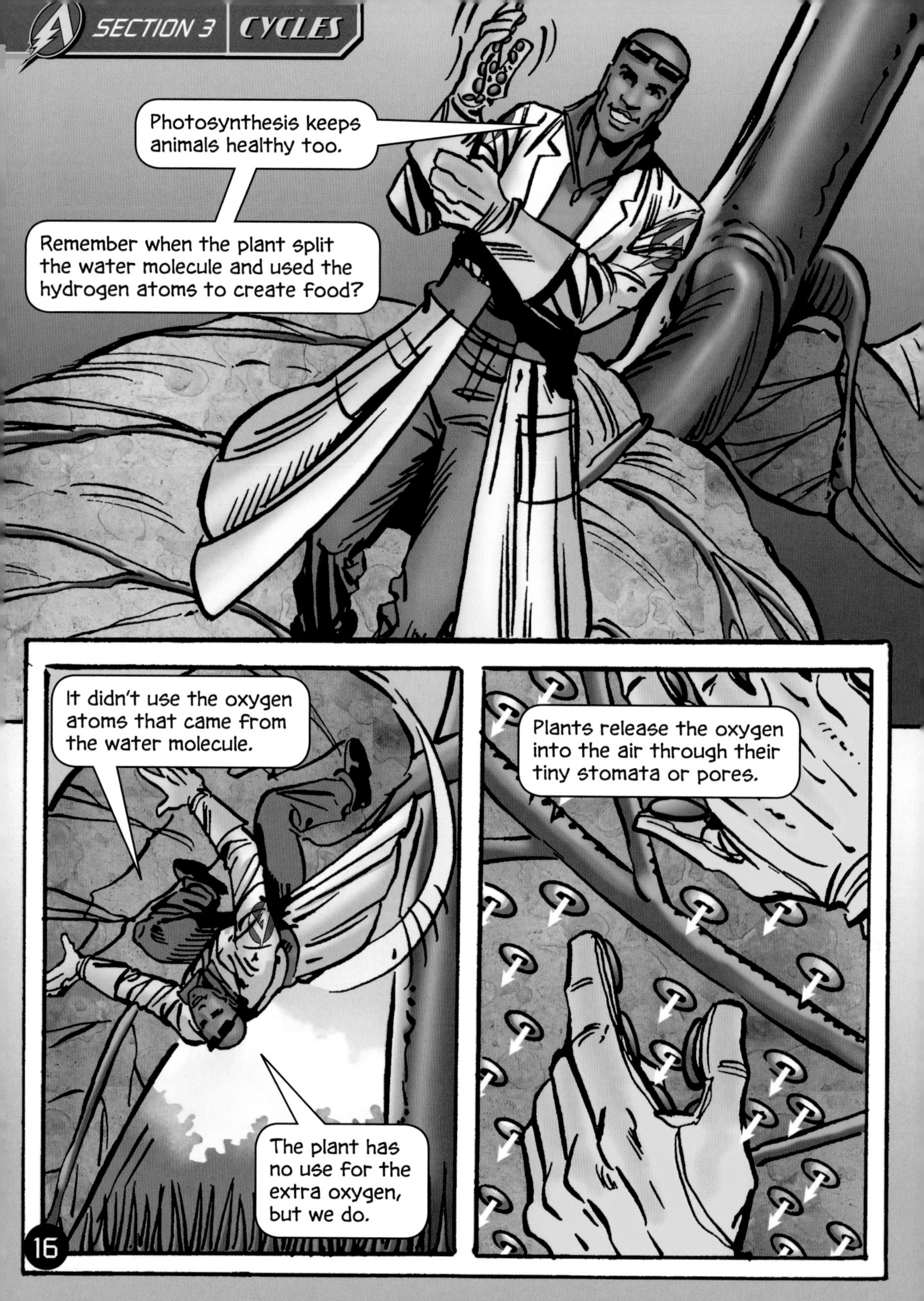
Photosynthesis keeps animals healthy too.
Remember when the plant split the water molecule and used the hydrogen atoms to create food?
It didn't use the oxygen atoms that came from the water molecule.
The plant has no use for the extra oxygen, but we do.
Plants release the oxygen into the air through their tiny stomata or pores.

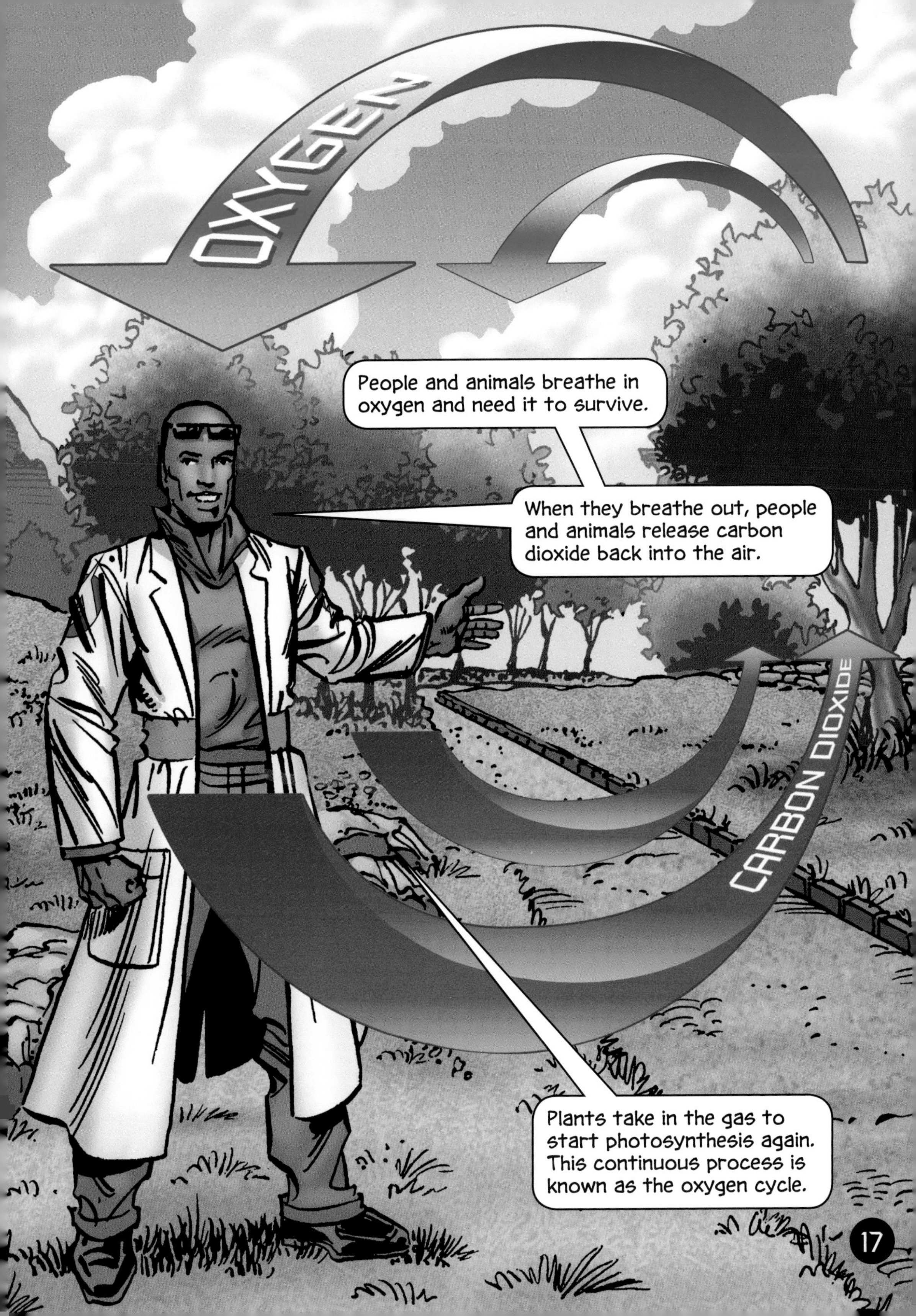
OXYGEN
People and animals breathe in oxygen and need it to survive.
When they breathe out, people and animals release carbon dioxide back into the air.
CARBON DIOXIDE
Plants take in the gas to start photosynthesis again. This continuous process is known as the oxygen cycle.

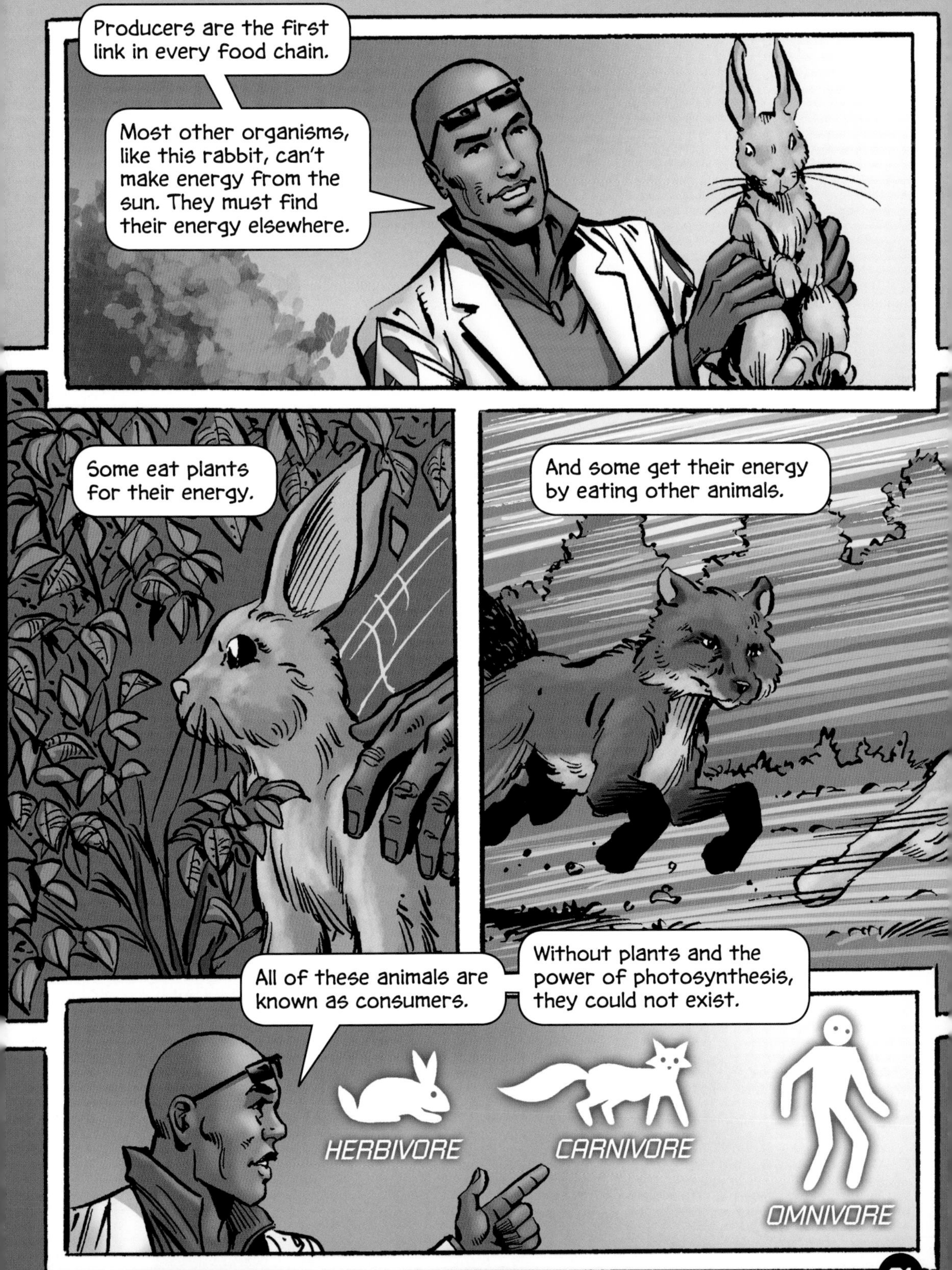

Producers are the first link in every food chain.
Most other organisms, like this rabbit, can't make energy from the sun. They must find their energy elsewhere.
Some eat plants for their energy.
And some get their energy by eating other animals.
All of these animals are known as consumers.
Without plants and the power of photosynthesis, they could not exist.
HERBIVORE
CARNIVORE
OMNIVORE

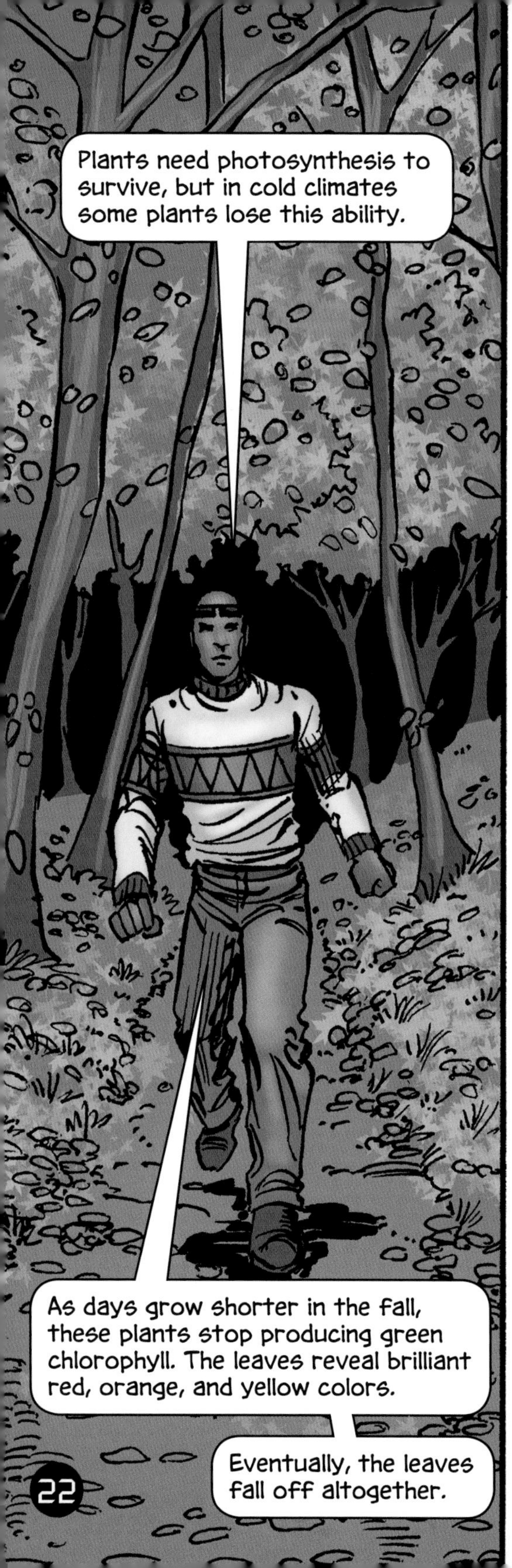

Plants need photosynthesis to survive, but in cold climates some plants lose this ability.
As days grow shorter in the fall, these plants stop producing green chlorophyll. The leaves reveal brilliant red, orange, and yellow colors.
Eventually, the leaves fall off altogether.

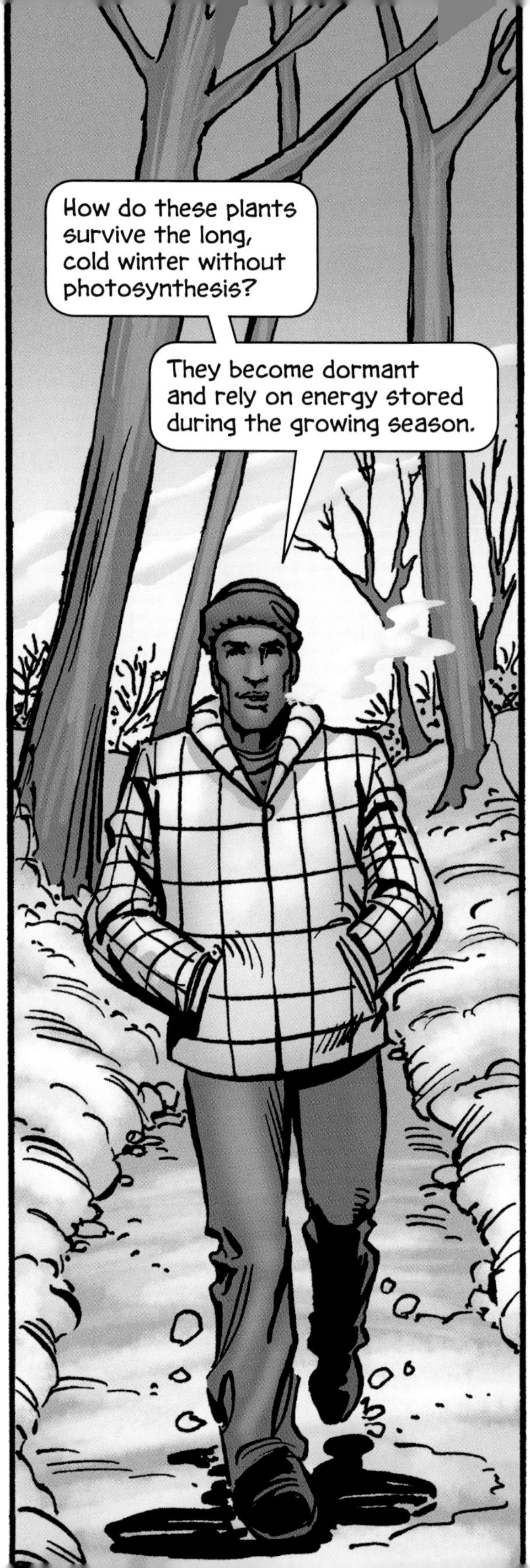

How do these plants survive the long, cold winter without photosynthesis?
They become dormant and rely on energy stored during the growing season.

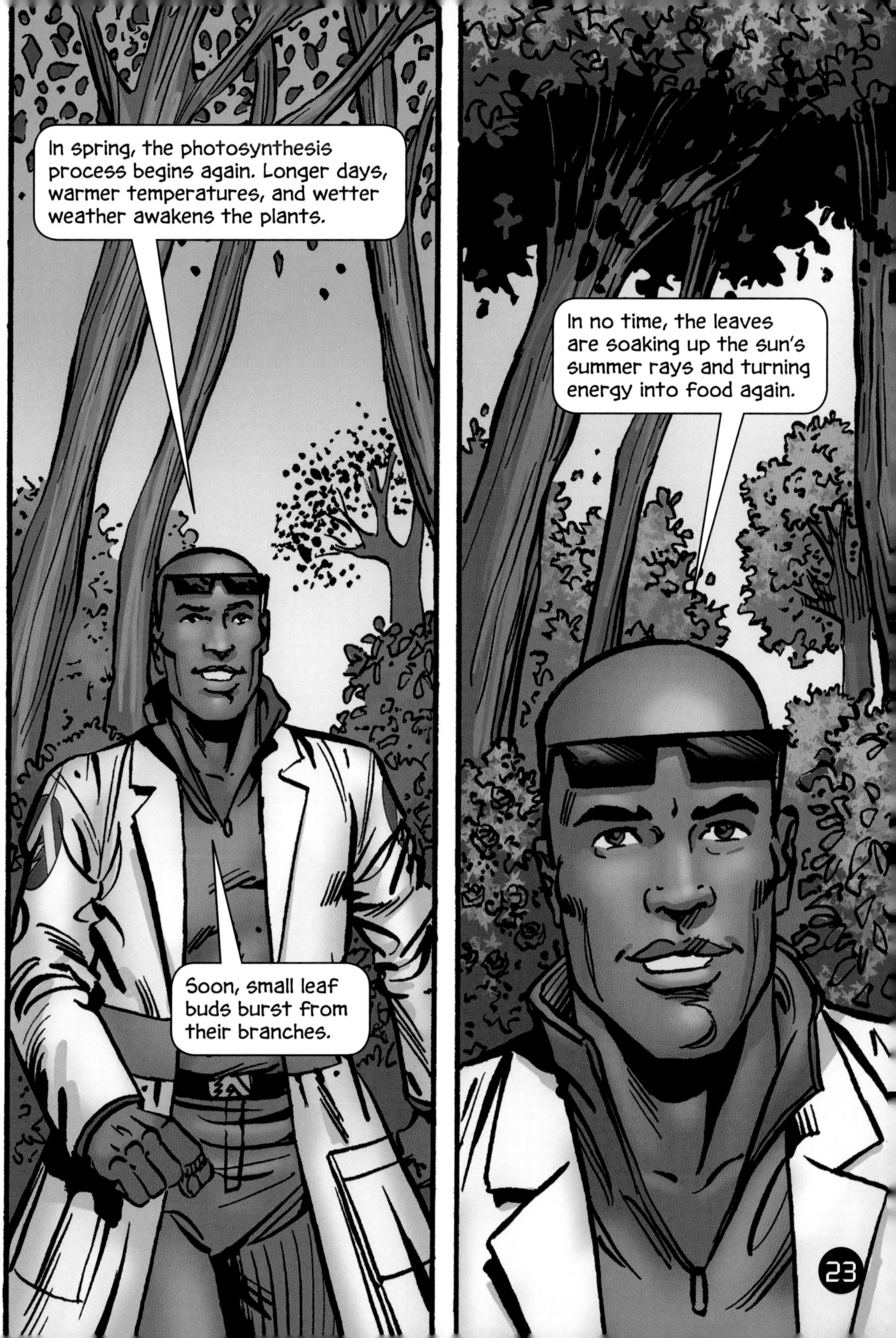
In spring, the photosynthesis process begins again. Longer days, warmer temperatures, and wetter weather awakens the plants.
Soon, small leaf buds burst from their branches.
In no time, the leaves are soaking up the sun's summer rays and turning energy into food again.

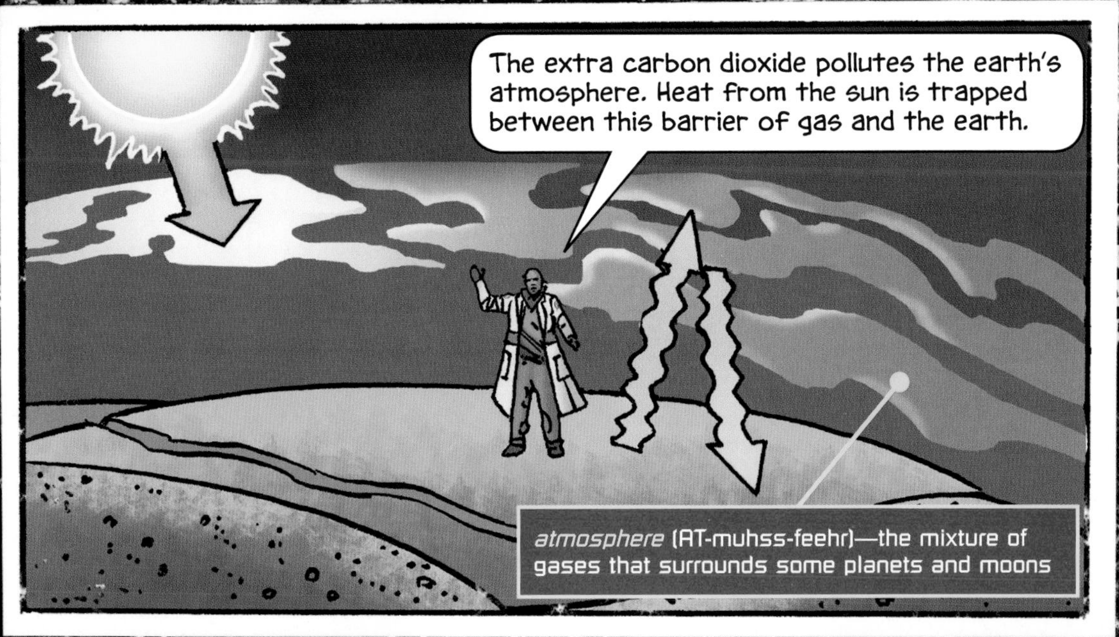
The extra carbon dioxide pollutes the earth's atmosphere. Heat from the sun is trapped between this barrier of gas and the earth.
atmosphere (AT-muhss-feehr)—the mixture of gases that surrounds some planets and moons

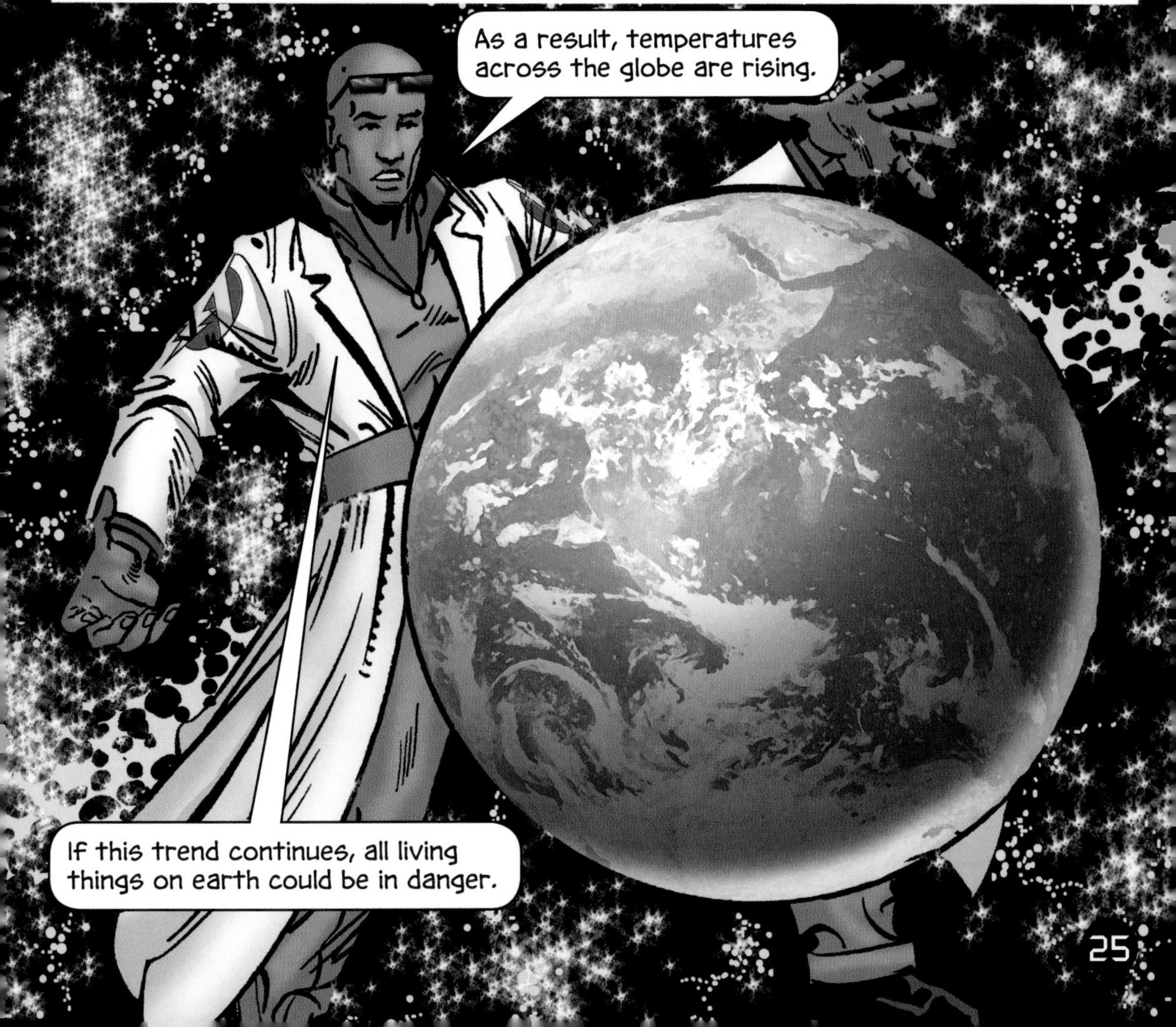
As a result, temperatures across the globe are rising.
If this trend continues, all living things on earth could be in danger.

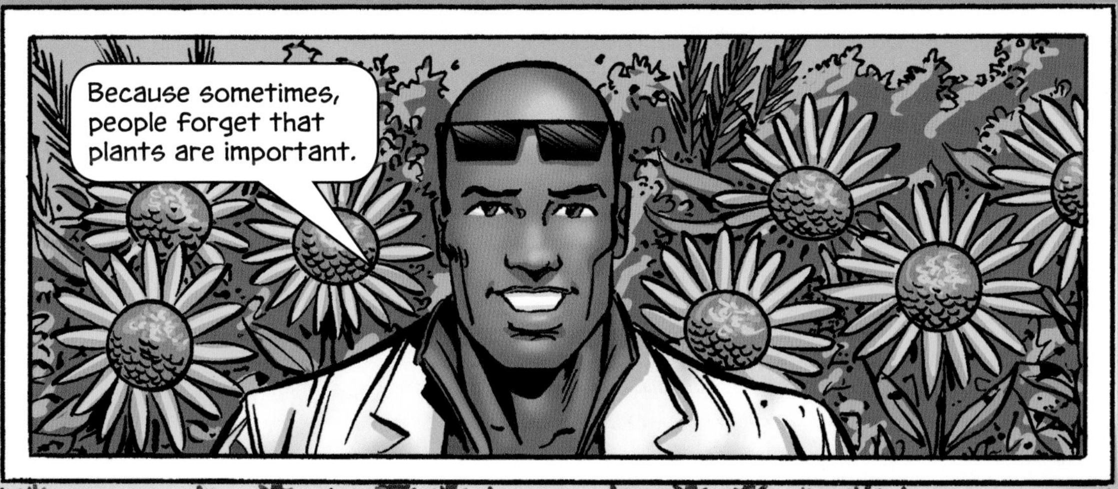
Because sometimes, people forget that plants are important.

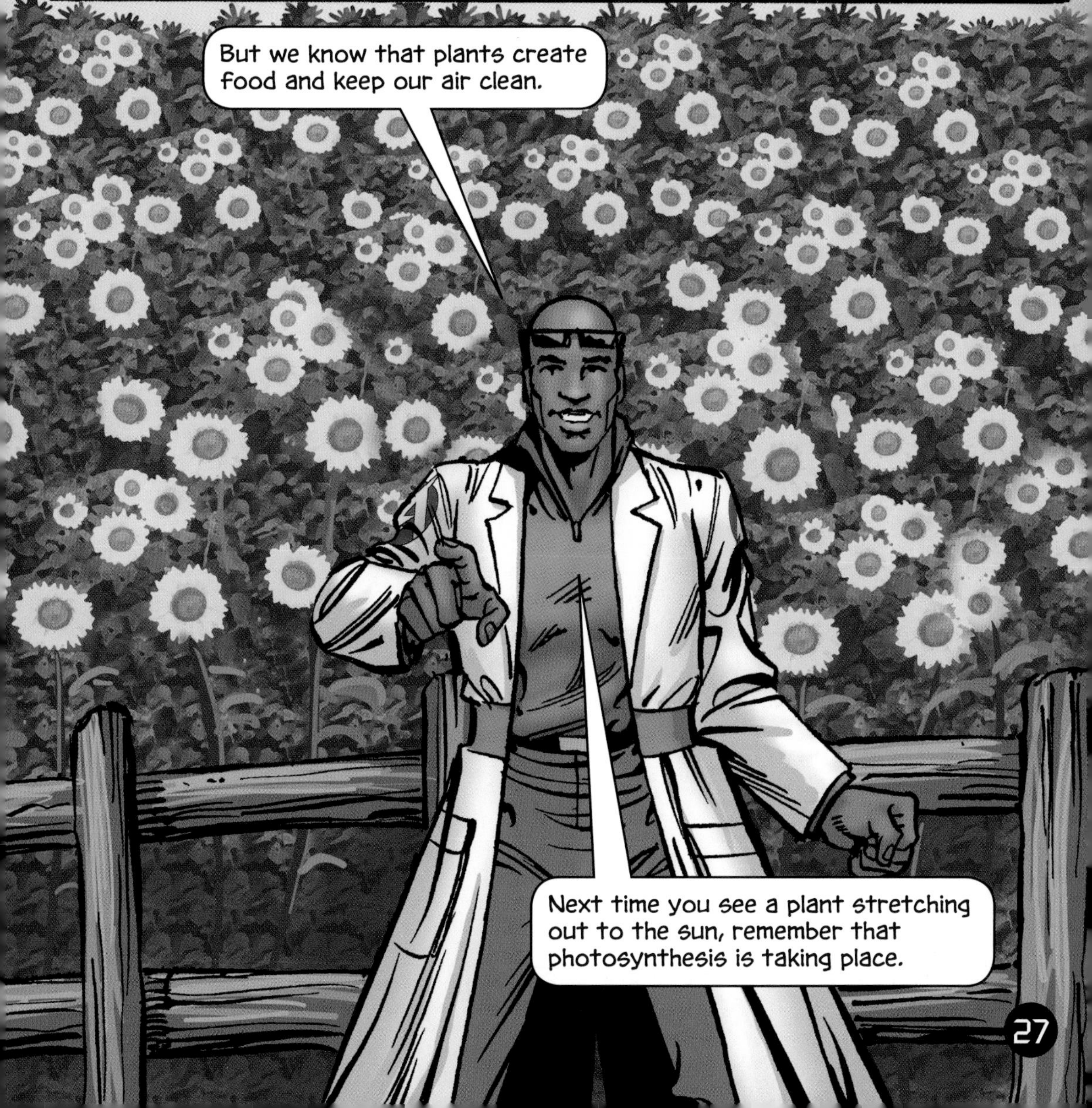
But we know that plants create food and keep our air clean.
Next time you see a plant stretching out to the sun, remember that photosynthesis is taking place.

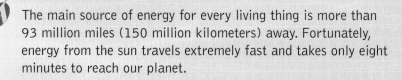
PHOTOSYNTHESIS

The main source of energy for every living thing is more than 93 million miles (150 million kilometers) away. Fortunately, energy from the sun travels extremely fast and takes only eight minutes to reach our planet.

Parts of the photosynthesis process can continue even without light from the sun. When the sun sets, plants still turn energy into sugars for food. This part of the process is known as the dark reaction phase.

Our planet has a wide variety of plant life. In fact, more than 260,000 species of plants grow on earth.

The Indian pipe plant has no chlorophyll. The flowering plant is completely white and has been called corpse plant or ghost flower. Lacking the ability to create food, the Indian pipe absorbs energy through its roots from fungi.

While some plants don't need sunlight, others don't need soil. Epiphyte plants dig their roots into trees or rocks for support. Moss, orchids, and other epiphytes often live high up on trees for better sunlight. Because of their location, they are sometimes called "air plants."

Planting a tree can have a major impact. One grown tree produces enough oxygen to support four people for a year.

Plants are the earth's only producers. Most other organisms are divided into three types of consumers:

Herbivores—animals that eat only plants
Carnivores—animals that eat other animals
Omnivores—animals that eat both plants and animals

 Plants can be carnivores. Some plants, including Venus flytraps and monkey cups, live where few nutrients are in the soil. They capture insects in their traps for food.

MORE ABOUT

SUPER SCIENTIST

Real name: Maxwell J. Axiom
Hometown: Seattle, Washington
Height: 6' 1"   Weight: 192 lbs
Eyes: Brown   Hair: None

Super capabilities: Super intelligence; able to shrink to the size of an atom; sunglasses give x-ray vision; lab coat allows for travel through time and space.

Origin: Since birth, Max Axiom seemed destined for greatness. His mother, a marine biologist, taught her son about the mysteries of the sea. His father, a nuclear physicist and volunteer park ranger, schooled Max on the wonders of earth and sky.

One day on a wilderness hike, a megacharged lightning bolt struck Max with blinding fury. When he awoke, Max discovered a newfound energy and set out to learn as much about science as possible. He traveled the globe earning degrees in every aspect of the field. Upon his return, he was ready to share his knowledge and new identity with the world. He had become Max Axiom, Super Scientist.

GLOSSARY

atmosphere (AT-muhss-feehr)—the mixture of gases that surrounds earth

atom (AT-uhm)—an element in its smallest form

carbon dioxide (KAHR-buhn dye-AHK-side)—a colorless, odorless gas that people and animals breathe out

chlorophyll (KLOER-uh-fil)—the green substance in plants that uses light to make food from carbon dioxide and water

hydrogen (HYE-druh-juhn)—a colorless gas that is lighter than air and burns easily

molecule (MOL-uh-kyool)—the atoms making up the smallest unit of a substance; H_2O is a molecule of water.

oxygen (OK-suh-juhn)—a colorless gas in the air that people and animals need to breathe

precipitation (pri-sip-i-TAY-shuhn)—water that falls from clouds to the earth's surface; precipitation can be rain, hail, sleet, or snow.

transpiration (transs-puh-RAY-shuhn)—the process by which plants give off moisture into the atmosphere

vascular (VASS-kew-luhr)—a system of channels for transporting fluids through plants

READ MORE

Biskup, Agnieszka. *Exploring Ecosystems with Max Axiom.* Graphic Science. Mankato, Minn.: Capstone Press, 2007.

Harman, Rebecca. *The Water Cycle.* Heinemann Infosearch. Chicago: Heinemann Library, 2005.

Juettner, Bonnie. *Photosynthesis.* The KidHaven Science Library. Detroit: KidHaven Press, 2005.

Kalman, Bobbie. *Food Chains and You.* Food Chains. New York: Crabtree, 2005.

Staub, Frank J. *Photosynthesis.* World of Wonder. Mankato, Minn.: Creative Education, 2003.

INTERNET SITES

FactHound offers a safe, fun way to find Internet sites related to this book. All of the sites on FactHound have been researched by our staff.

Here's how:
1. Visit *www.facthound.com*
2. Choose your grade level.
3. Type in this book ID **0736868410** for age-appropriate sites. You may also browse subjects by clicking on letters, or by clicking on pictures and words.
4. Click on the **Fetch It** button.

FactHound will fetch the best sites for you!

Index

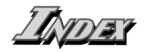